Eclectica, Volume 1

Business Advice from an Artist

By Deepak Morris

with foreward by Cyril Desbruslais, sj

Edited by Aaron Brachfeld

ISBN-13: 978-1519796684

ISBN-10: 1519796684

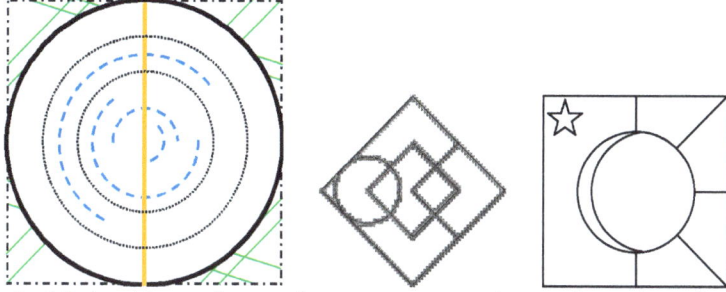

Published by Loka Hatha Yoga in Castle Rock, Colorado

There are many suitable places for your meditation.
We hope this becomes one of them.
Anguttara Nikaya 1.159

LOKAHATHAYOGA@GMAIL.COM - (719) 422-9536
http://lokareview.blogspot.com/p/books.html
lokahathayoga.blogspot.com

AUTHOR'S DEDICATION:

To the Universe, which birthed me into a family of witty individuals and sent me to schools that challenged the heaven out of me.

ABOUT THE AUTHOR

If asked to describe himself in just one word, Deepak would use a compound one, non-conformist. Deepak has never coloured inside the lines, always seeking new ways to do things. Even his art teacher in school was rather taken aback – even if not impressed – by the way Deepak dealt with art techniques. If he didn't like the techniques taught to him, he invented new ones.

Coming from a family of avid readers, Deepak soon discovered the joys of sinking into a good book and was soon far outstripping his classmates, both in choice of reading material and speed of reading. Deepak figuratively devoured books like a gourmand, reading anything and everything. One of his chief delights at the start of school was to read all his textbooks for the academic year as if they were novels, mostly cover to cover in about an hour each.

Developing thus an eclectic interest in just about everything – he has authored over a dozen guide books on management subjects ranging from Business Ethics to Marketing to Information Technology, has been published in the Chicken Soup for the Indian Soul series and has written and staged over forty musicals – en route collecting a Master's Degree in Commerce, a Master's Diploma in Management, an International Diploma in Computer Studies and an International Professional Certificate in Communication, Deepak has developed a succinct style that addresses the root of intellect as well as emotion.

He currently lives in Pune, India, teaching Speech, Drama and Communication, and writing and staging musicals – book and lyrics – for schools.

TABLE OF CONTENTS

Forward – by Cyril Desbruslais, sj

In the beginning was the word. And the word was filled with power. And he who knew how to make and use words had access to power.

Words are currency, like Pounds, Euros, Dollars . . . and Rupees. And he who has a bigger vocabulary is, in a very real sense, richer than one who has a smaller one, just as he who has more money is wealthier than he who has little. Words may not necessarily get you many things, but - if you know how to use them well - can get you lots of power, power over the minds and hearts of people whom you can persuade to help you realise your projects.

Deepak Morris is one of those persons; who knows his words, possesses a rich supply of them and knows how to mould and meld them for noble purposes. No ruthless demagogue is he, luring people into all kinds of quicksand by the pleasing sirens with which he serenades them. Rather, he provokes you to think and reflect, prior to action, whether you would always agree with him or not. I don't, but he always makes me pause to critically consider.

I've known Deepak Morris for literally decades, as animator of a youth group with which he has been associated, on and off, for about thirty years. I've seen him grow from a somewhat shy, introvert schoolboy into a full-fledged, confident leader, not afraid to stand out as not being quite "one of the crowd". I've heard him debate, read many of his well thought-out pieces of writing and sat through some of his many thought-provoking plays. I know him as a skilled instructor in public speaking and a proficient emcee in many contexts. Indeed he has, more than once, tutored Miss India finalists on how to use words to impress their judges.

This armoury/treasury of Deepak's words is primarily addressed to business people. But lesser mortals, like myself, will feel themselves enriched after having gone through them, even if one cannot totally agree with a particular comment here and there. And one cannot deny that it is always well said and provides ample food for thought. Happy reading!

Cyril Desbruslais sj
Pune, India

Cyril Desbruslais is a Jesuit in Pune, with a Ph.D. from the Sorbonne, France. He is an expert on the Bible, having read it in the original Greek. His sermons attract international audiences but he continues to work among the youth in Pune, sure that his work will have universal repercussions.

No one cares what you're offering. Everyone is looking for what they're seeking. Get this and you'll be a master marketer - - -

I love my Mondays - - -

I never suffer from Monday Morning Blues. How can I?
How can I be blue about doing the things I love?

The way to be better than good - - -

You can't just be good - you have to be fantastically good.
The only way to be fantastically good is to be passionate
about what you do. Being passionate involves risking
making a fool of yourself in public. Do you have what it
takes to be laughed at and still carry on?

Be interesting! - - -

When God was handing out earthly lives, I found the line
for "Comfortable" too long and the line for "Successful"
composed of people I'd rather not know. So I went to the
"Interesting" line and found all of you!

The purpose of life - - -

The purpose of life is to have fun. Have you had fun today?

A difference between grammar and writing - - -

Thousands of children are taught grammar. How many
become great writers? Only the passionate.

The myth of the struggling actor - - -

The Gulf Today
Thursday, March 20, 1997

The visit to be staged in Dubai

Actors from the Dubai Drama Group are preparing for their next performance, *The Visit*, which starts on Sunday.

BY A STAFF REPORTER

There is a myth that an actor cannot earn a regular income. Like most myths, it is fuelled by the examples of a few struggling actors. These, I submit, are the exception rather than the rule.

The very essence of acting is to be able to handle any role. Ergo, an actor can easily sustain the role of a paid employee. But there's even more, in case one thinks that sustaining the role of an employee is a dishonest way to earn money.

You see, an actor who's enthusiastic about acting gains a whole lot of experience in a whole lot of fields... public speaking, acting, teamwork and so on. The more enthusiastic even get trained in juggling, acrobatics, ventriloquism...

Far from being restricted to one field, an actor has training and expertise in several fields. Just training people in any of these fields can provide regular income to an actor, even if the actor does not actively pursue these fields.

When you are an actor, the world is your oyster... and theatre gives you plenty of tools to open that bivalve.

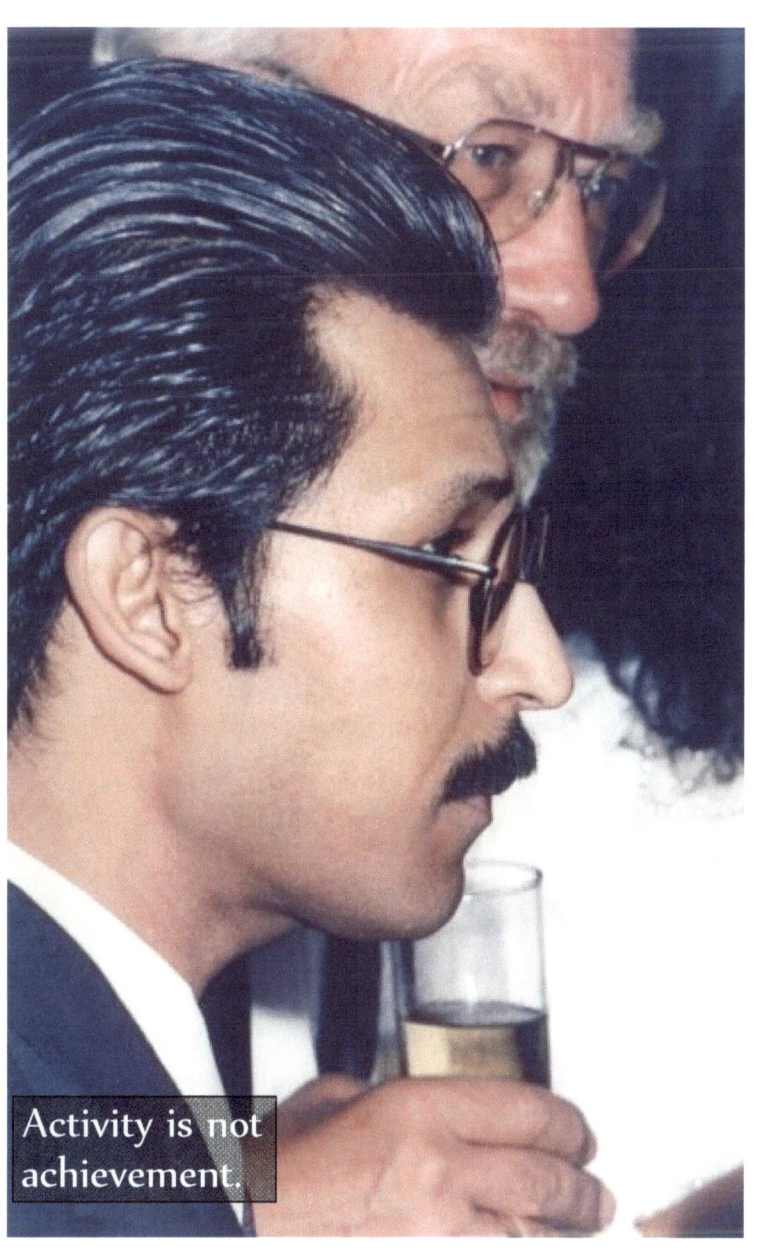

Activity is not achievement.

Literature helps us make decisions - - -

You're going to hate me for this but I hate Disney Corporation. I don't just dislike it, I hate it. Sure, it has awesome parks and rides and stuff (all paid for by you but you like it, so, well) but. I. Hate. How. It. Massacres. Classics.

Aladdin was not a thief. He wasn't even Middle-Eastern, he was Chinese! There was no Princess Jasmine in the original tale. Her name was Badr-al-badour and she had no pet tiger. Aladdin did not travel on a magic carpet. There is not a single mention of a magic carpet in the original tale. Those are just some of the major departures from the original tales that Disney Corp. decides to foist upon the audiences.

People might be inclined to say, "So what? An entertaining tale is an entertaining tale! What the oral tradition of the Arabian Nights did for its audiences, Disney Corp. does for a much larger audience, so all's good." The problem is, in its desire to make profit, Disney Corporation cares a hang for the morality sought to be taught by the tales it re-tells. It ends up telling people that being a thief is good, it gets you the Princess. It scarcely touches upon the moral dilemmas that classic literature seeks to examine.

It divides decisions into black and white and good literature has never attempted to do that. Good literature always makes one question every decision, sometimes to the point of not being able to make a decision. That's not a bad.

When, in my dramatic adaptation of Treasure Island, I am asked if "Yo-ho-ho and a bottle of rum" can be changed to "yo-ho-ho and a bottle of juice", it incenses me that some righteous people think children are incapable of discerning between right and wrong. Children are QUITE capable of seeing that the very drinking of alcohol might turn a man violent.

We do not protect children by shielding them from violence. We make them more vulnerable to it by not acknowledging its existence.

How to act - - -

I don't believe in acting on stage. Anyone can pretend to cry and mask his face and make sob noises. When an actor can summon tears simply by being the part... THAT is being, not acting. Anyone can act. Being requires a bigger skill set.

The value of work - - -

If I enjoy what I do, most people don't consider it "work," arguing that it's fun for me and therefore not "work." A hobby, perhaps, and therefore not payable. But if I'm delivering value, no matter how much I enjoy doing so, must I not be paid in cash?

Refuse to take offense - - -

It seems to me that all attempts at creating division fail when we refuse to take offence.

When I was in school, a bully said to me, "Christians rub their girlfriends in public."

He fully expected me to bristle (as I am Catholic and "Catholic" and "Christian" are one and the same to most in India and public displays of affection are more or less taboo here).

I nodded.

"Aren't you angry?" he asked.

"No, why should I be angry at anything you say? You can say what you want."

He kinda withdrew from the discussion.

You are you! - - -

You are you and you must do what you want to do or are called to do. You are not an artist or a businessperson or a housewife or a menial labourer, you are you!

What are you doing that you demand of you?

If you're on the wrong track, don't rush in your hurry to get back on the right track - - -

As the Talegaon local started the man opposite me looked at me in alarm.

"Isn't this the Nagercoil Express?" he asked, shaken out of his complacence since the said Express had to be travelling in the opposite direction.

"It's the Talegaon local", I replied, whereupon he hustled his pregnant wife, their infant daughter and two huge bags and signalled his intention to have the adult humans jump off the train, lugging baby and baggage.

Jumping off a local is not a recommended action, since the local is an EMU and picks up considerable speed within milliseconds.

It was the first time I saw almost all the occupants of a compartment on a local train join together to stop a man from committing a really foolish act. They made him stay put till the next station (just minutes away) and advised him to take an auto rickshaw back to Pune Railway Station, ask around and catch the right train.

A parable - - -

Saw a stray dog eagerly clamber up a pile of earth to bury a precious chicken leg bone in it and my heart just broke - the pile would be gone by the morrow, made part of a concrete wall.

Learn math so shopkeepers don't cheat you - - -

"Why do I have to learn multiplication tables when I'll never use them?" asked my student, all of 12.

"Don't you want to catch the local shopkeeper trying to cheat you by multiplying wrong?" [I know, it's "wrongly", but we'll let it go]

"They do that?" he asked in wonder.

"Everyone who can get away with it does it."

Disappointment is irrational - - -

If nothing works out the way you expect it should, it simply means you don't know shit.

Practice economy — even with vaccination - - -

Eat street food from the time you start attending school; get a bit sick, recover, develop immunity; eat street food as an adult; Rs.25 per plate.

Don't eat street food, get immunisation shots (Rs.10 to Rs.25 each), drink only bottled water (Rs.15 per litre); eat cosmetic street food as an adult at a mall; Rs.50 per plate - after you've spent Rs.15 per day for the last 15 years.

Doesn't quite make sense.

New work is the best work - - -

The most successful professionals are those that design their jobs. Think about it: Most guys originally cut their own hair and shaved their own beards. Some wiseacre stepped up and said, "Okay, guys, I'll cut your hair and shave you, you concentrate on sharpening your spear."
The barber was created.

Then someone said, "While that guy's shaving you, I can sharpen your spear so you can have a cup of tea." The spear/knife sharpener was created. Also the tea-shop.

What job will you design today?

Be willing to pay for quality - - -

Submitted my face to a barber's blade. I have to say, although it cost me the price of a Gillette Mach 3 cartridge that would have sufficed for a whole month, the experience was exhilarating and the result, a face so smooth, girls would die to rub against it. Next date, preparation will involve a barber's shave for sure!

Be not in need - - -

When you are centred, there is no NEED. You might enjoy food but you do not crave it. If you are hungry, it makes no difference. If you are vegetarian, you feel no superiority over non-vegetarians. If you are non-vegetarian, you feel no antagonism towards vegetarians. You understand that all is as it should be.

How to be mind-fuck proof - - -

Don't try to mind-fuck me, I don't have a mind.

Take hope: success is actually quite easy - - -

Read one of the early Perry Mason novels. Gives me hope that I shall one day be able to write a novel, since it was pure bull crap in plot and treatment and not at all like Gardner's later polished pieces.

Be patient and learn until you're ready - - -

Peevish actors drop out of plays after being told they are not yet ready. Real actors keep at it until they are ready. When people drop out of my productions I take consolation in the fact that there are people like Leon who are willing to do what it takes to become actors.

For his first production, Leon was a gopher, even though he was the son of a rich man. He attended rehearsals faithfully and even fetched mosquito repellant for cast and crew.

In his second production, he played a non-speaking role, remaining silently on stage, doing what he had to do, reacting to every nuance of other actors.

In subsequent productions I gave him speaking roles and he ran the gamut from comedy to intense emotion, finally delivering a performance that would be hard to beat in "The Patriarch", a murder mystery in which he played a police inspector whose love was trapped in a loveless marriage.

I might not be much but if, on my deathbed, I think back on people I admire, Larry is certainly one of them.

I cannot, of course, forget Naina, who stepped in just a couple of days from show date to play Malaika in "Business Is War" at the NDA.

It is people like these who tell me that, no matter how disappointed I might get with humans, there are some who make the living worthwhile.

The difference between Art and the Artiste - - -

The greatest artists create because they cannot suffer the boredom of doing anything else. True, Shakespeare wrote and staged to stave off starvation but he could easily have become a teacher, and think how boring that would have been for him. And so he created works that teach long after his death.

Glory dies with the artiste.

Art lives long after the artist is gone.

Being the best – not being better - - -

You can strive to be the best or you can try to pull others down. Guess which approach works the best?

If you want to lead, lead. Blocking others is not leading. Be focused on leading, not blocking. Leaders lead, losers block.

Set your schedule based upon who you are - - -

So this parent called a teacher I work with to ask if I'd teach her son on an exclusive basis daily.

"What time would you want Deepak to be there?" she (the teacher) asked.

"7:45 am", replied the parent.

"Forget it, Deepak's a bachelor and goes to sleep at 7 am."

I love people who get me

A bully ignored
soon loses their
power - - -

We learn from our elders what to do - - -

Why do we like stories from our elders?

I think there is a deep human need to know where we came from and why we are here. We perhaps believe or desire that, by learning of times before we were born from those immediately around us, we will somehow know or learn what we are to do.

I loved my Grandma's and aunt's and dad's and uncles' stories of their childhood and things they did. Even Mum told me of her naughty brother's escapades and I delighted in them.

My students also want to know about my past. What it was like when I was young and there was no TV or mobile phone. Far from me boasting about a glorious past, they ask about silly things I or people around me might have done.

How to always know what to do - - -

"How can you see action when the script indicates none?" I was asked.

"Mostly, I've been there, done that. I know from experience." I replied.

"You CANNOT have been in a leaky boat in the middle of a lake, unable to swim!"

"I have been in a boat in the middle of a lake and my imagination supplied the rest, " I replied.

I see no reason
why we can't trust
each other. Hurt is
no excuse - - -

Find your motivation - - -

Manchu's Biryani is good. A very good meal for Rs.100. I started off thinking I'd have half the Biryani for lunch and the rest for dinner but wound up eating it all at lunch.

I need to make more money.

Get the education you need to succeed - - -

Education in modern society is skewed to weirdness, in my opinion.

Why are we putting children through a patterned education when history has shown that thinking outside the box makes for greatest wealth?

The ones who have the most wealth generated within a lifetime are those who fleece the sheeple. Why are we creating sheeple for fleecing, rather blithely?

Every skill has multiple applications — and can make a party better - - -

A ten-year-old girl delivered a set of steps to organise a party that a programmer would be proud to deliver. I asked her if she had learned computer programming. "No Sir," she said, "My daddy taught me." Her father owns a software company. A warm glow engulfed me when I thought how her certainly busy father took the time to teach her to be logical.

Thinking is work, too - - -

www.ingramcontent.com/pod-product-compliance
Lightning Source LLC
Chambersburg PA
CBHW041211180526
45172CB00006B/1233